Super
Story-Writing
Strategies
&
Activities

by Barbara Mariconda and Dea Paoletta Auray

SCHOLASTIC
PROFESSIONALBOOKS

NEW YORK • TORONTO • LONDON • AUCKLAND • SYDNEY
MEXICO CITY • NEW DELHI • HONG KONG

To Sam, Stacie, and Peter
for making hard work fun.

Cover design by Jaime Lucero
Cover illustration by Lynne Cravath
Interior design by Solutions by Design
Interior illustrations by Delana Bettoli

ISBN: 0-439-14008-0

INTRODUCTION 4

HOW TO USE THIS BOOK 5

STORY BEGINNINGS
Getting Started 6
Active Beginnings 7
"Hey!" "What?" "Oh, no!" 8
Thoughts and Feelings 9
Did You Hear Something? 10
Smorgasbord 11
Author's Choice 12

SENTENCE VARIETY
Getting Started 13
Separating the Grocery List 14
Fixing the Broken Record 19
Changing the Subject 22

DESCRIPTIONS THAT DAZZLE!
Getting Started 27
Paint a Picture 28
Sensory Sentence-Starter Chart 33
Sensory Sentence-Starters 34
Use Your Senses 36

SMOOTH TRANSITIONS
Getting Started 38
Red Flag Menu 39
Warning! Red Flags 40

MAIN EVENT
Getting Started 43
Builders and Stretchers 44

DIALOGUE AND THOUGHT
Getting Started 49
Too Much Talk 50
All Thought, No Action 53

STORY ENDINGS
Getting Started 55
End With Style 56
Start an Ending 58
Take Your Pick 59

STORY ANALYSIS AND REVISION
Getting Started 61
"The Wizard in the Cave" (Sample Story) 62
Analyze This Story! 63
"The Wizard in the Cave" (Sample Revision) 64

Young writers have boundless imaginations and wonderful ideas, which can lead to fantastic story-writing. However, they are often overwhelmed by the task of getting their ideas onto the page. Instead of elaborating on the important parts of their stories, children often resort to summarizing. They frequently get stuck in transitions or bogged down with dialogue and plot. How can we get students unstuck and on their way to great writing? The dozens of reproducibles in this book teach kids surefire techniques that will give them a jump start in the story-writing process.

The techniques described in this book are designed to help children overcome typical pitfalls in their writing. Each technique is described in a short Writer's Tip at the top of the reproducible. A clear example demonstrates how to use the skill. Then students practice using these skills as they revise sample writing. You'll find reproducibles that help kids learn to:

- Jump-start a story beginning

- Vary sentence structure

- Describe using the five senses

- Break down the "grocery list" (*The frog was big, green, slippery, and wet.*)

- Replace the "broken record" (*He had brown hair. He had blue eyes. He had fuzzy eyebrows.*)

- Achieve sentence variety through a subject shift and the use of active verbs (*He wore a red coat* becomes *A red coat hugged his large frame.*)

- Use specific adjectives instead of general adjectives

- Move plots forward using transitional "red flag" phrases (*Suddenly…, Just then…, The next thing I knew…*)

- Elaborate on the main event using action, exclamation, dialogue, thoughts, feelings, and sounds

- Turn "too much talk" into action or description

- Wrap up stories with style

This book is divided into eight sections, with an introductory teacher's page for each. The introductory pages define, discuss, and illustrate the writing strategies covered in each section. Be sure to read "How to Use These Materials" on page 5 to get the most out of these activities. We are confident that you will find these activities to be helpful, easy to use, and exactly what you need to help your students get their plots unstuck and their ideas fully expressed!

Happy writing!
Barbara Mariconda and Dea Paoletta Auray

How can you help your students get the most out of the activities in this book? Modeling the writing process for students is the best way to empower them as writers. However, this requires that the teacher prepare in advance so that he or she knows both the questions to ask and the direction the writing will take. A helpful resource for lessons and activities is *The Most Wonderful Writing Lessons Ever* (Scholastic Teaching Strategies, 1999).

Here are the steps we suggest to produce the best results:

1 Getting Started

Use the introductory page at the beginning of each section to define and introduce a particular writing strategy to the class. Show students the examples provided so that they can see how the strategy is used.

2 Model the Strategy for the Class

Choose an activity sheet to use as a demonstration. First, reproduce the sheet for each student or make a transparency to use on an overhead projector. Walk students through the activity by thinking aloud and asking for suggestions when appropriate. In this way, you are essentially demonstrating an author's thought processes while writing.

3 Guided Practice

A number of similar activity sheets for each writing strategy provide plenty of opportunities for modeling and guided practice. We have found that students become comfortable with a writing technique by working through a number of similar exercises, and that they truly grow proficient through repeated practice. Distribute the same or a similar activity page to students, and have them work independently or cooperatively in small groups. Circulate through the classroom offering assistance, encouragement, and positive feedback.

Repeat Steps 1–3 several times before moving on to the last step, application.

4 Application

After you have introduced and modeled a particular skill, you may assign similar activities to be completed independently, in small cooperative groups, or as a whole class. You may also choose certain activities for mini-lessons for select groups of students based on assessed needs. A combination of these experiences is often helpful for students.

Have students write a story or part of a story to allow them to apply a particular skill to their own writing. For example, have them write just a beginning of a story to practice the strategies in the first section. It is helpful for students to apply one skill at a time to shorter writing assignments. As students become more proficient, assign longer pieces.

Getting Started

The first line or two of a story is perhaps the most important part. If the very beginning doesn't grab the reader's attention, he or she is likely to put it down. Readers are impatient with stories that begin slowly or that are generally predictable and dull. Student writers are often unsure about how to begin a story, and so they fall into a number of patterns that do not produce the desired effect.

For example:

> *Once upon a time…*
> *This is my story about…*
> *Hi! My name is…*
> *One sunny day…*

How can kids jump-start their stories in ways that will grab the reader's attention? They can use a number of effective techniques that published authors use:

Have the main character…

DO SOMETHING

Put the character in the setting doing something relevant to the story. For example, begin a camping story in the woods with the main character setting up a tent.

> *I hiked to the clearing and found the perfect spot for my tent.*

SAY SOMETHING
(exclamation or dialogue)

Begin by having the main character say something relevant to the story.

> *"This is the perfect spot to set up the tent!" I said as I headed into the clearing.*

THINK OR FEEL

Begin with the main character's thoughts or feelings about something important in the story.

> *I wonder if I'll meet any wild animals out here, I thought as I set up my tent in the clearing.*

HEAR A SOUND

Use a sound to draw the reader into the setting or action.

> *Crunch! Crunch! The leaves on the forest floor crackled beneath my feet as I hiked toward the clearing to set up camp.*

Notice that in each example, the author sets a purpose (camping) and establishes the setting (a clearing in the forest). The story begins as close to the main event as possible—it does not begin with the character at home, waking up, getting dressed, having breakfast, or driving to the forest. In this way, the reader is plunged right into the story.

The activity pages in this section of the book are set up as revision exercises. Students are given a "boring" beginning to revise using the techniques listed above. Explain that the story beginning must capture the reader's attention quickly and that authors use action, dialogue, thoughts, feelings, or sounds to do this. Model one of these revision exercises for students, and discuss a variety of choices that work. Then have students, either individually or as a whole class, try some of the activity pages. Remind students that they are only writing the beginning—not an entire story—and that it should consist of only a sentence or two!

Name _____   Date _____

Active Beginnings

✏️ **Writer's Tip:** In order to capture your reader's attention, the beginning of your story must be interesting and lively enough to make your reader want to keep reading. One way to do this is to begin with an action.

DIRECTIONS: Revise each story beginning. Put your main character in the setting, and have the character do something relevant to the story.

> EXAMPLE: *One rainy day I went to the mall.*

> REVISION: *I splashed across the parking lot, yanked open the tall glass door, and, dripping wet, stepped into the mall.*

1 **Hi. My name is Kate. This is a story about the time I went to the zoo.**
Put Kate (main character) at the zoo (setting) doing something (action).

REVISION: _____

_____

_____

2 **This is a story about the time I built a robot in my basement.**
Put yourself (main character) in the basement (setting) doing something (action).

REVISION: _____

_____

_____

3 **I will tell you about my adventure swimming at the lake.**
Put yourself (main character) at the lake (setting) doing something (action).

REVISION: _____

_____

_____

Name _____ Date _____

"Hey!" "What?" "Oh, no!"

Writer's Tip: In order to capture your reader's attention, the beginning of your story must be interesting and lively enough to make your reader want to keep reading. One way to do this is to begin with an exclamation.

Directions: Revise each story beginning. Think about what your main character might exclaim in each situation. (Remember to use quotation marks around what is being said.)

Example: *One rainy day I went to the mall.*

Revision: *"I'm soaked!" I yelled as I reached for the large glass mall entrance doors.*

1 **Hi. My name is Kate. This is a story about the time I went to the zoo.**
What might Kate exclaim at the zoo?

Revision: _____

_____

_____

2 **This is a story about the time I built a robot in my basement.**
Imagine that you are in the basement building a robot. What might you exclaim?

Revision: _____

_____

_____

3 **I will tell you about my swimming adventure at the lake.**
You are at the lake. What might you say?

Revision: _____

_____

_____

Name _____ Date _____

Thoughts and Feelings

Writer's Tip: In order to capture your reader's attention, the beginning of your story must be interesting and lively enough to make your reader want to keep reading. One way to do this is to begin with the main character's thoughts or feelings.

DIRECTIONS: Revise each story beginning. Start the story by describing the thoughts or feelings of the main character.

EXAMPLE: *One rainy day I went to the mall.*

REVISION: *As I approached the mall, I nervously glanced at my watch and wondered what my first day on the job would be like.*

1 **Hi. My name is Kate. This is a story about the time I went to the zoo.**
What might Kate think or feel as she approaches the zoo?

REVISION: _____

_____

_____

2 **This is a story about the time I built a robot in my basement.**
Imagine that you are building a robot. What might you think or feel?

REVISION: _____

_____

_____

3 **I will tell you about my swimming adventure at the lake.**
You are at the lake. What might you think or feel?

REVISION: _____

_____

_____

Name _____ Date _____

Did You Hear Something?

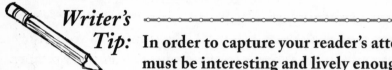

Writer's Tip: In order to capture your reader's attention, the beginning of your story must be interesting and lively enough to make your reader want to keep reading. One way to do this is to begin with a sound.

DIRECTIONS: Revise each story beginning. Start the story with an attention-grabbing sound. (Be sure that the sound is relevant to the story.)

EXAMPLE: *One rainy day I went to the mall.*

REVISION: *Splish! Splash! My boots sloshed through the puddles as I ran for the mall entrance.*

1 **Hi. My name is Kate. This is a story about the time I went to the zoo.**
What might Kate hear at the zoo?

REVISION: _____

_____

_____

2 **This is a story about the time I built a robot in my basement.**
Imagine that you are in the basement building a robot. What sounds might you hear?

REVISION: _____

_____

_____

3 **I will tell you about my swimming adventure at the lake.**
You are at the lake. What sounds might you hear?

REVISION: _____

_____

_____

Super Story-Writing Strategies & Activities Scholastic Professional Books

Name _____   Date _____

Smorgasbord

Writer's Tip: Authors usually try several story beginnings before they decide which one works best. Starting with action, exclamation, dialogue, thoughts, feelings, and sounds are some of the techniques authors use.

DIRECTIONS: Revise the story beginning by using each of the four techniques: action, exclamation or dialogue, thoughts or feelings, and sound. Then circle the revision that you feel works best.

Hello. This is my story about meeting a troll while hiking in the woods.

1 Revise this beginning using an action. What would you be doing as you begin your hike in the woods?

_____

_____

2 Revise this beginning using an exclamation. What might you say as you begin your hike in the woods?

_____

_____

3 Revise this beginning using a thought or feeling. What might you think about or how might you feel as you begin your hike in the woods?

_____

_____

4 Revise this beginning using a sound. What might you hear as you begin your hike in the woods?

_____

_____

Name _____ Date _____

Author's Choice

 *Writer's Tip:* Once an author has mastered the various techniques for starting stories effectively, he or she must decide which technique works best in a given story. Will an action be more exciting than a sound? Will dialogue add a funny touch or set the tone for a spine-tingling tale? Will thoughts and feelings reveal something about an amazing, unusual character? It's the author's choice!

Dɪʀᴇᴄᴛɪᴏɴꜱ: Revise each story beginning. Choose the technique (action, exclamation or dialogue, thoughts or feelings, or sound) that works best for each example given. You may want to try several techniques to find the one that works best.

1 One sunny day I went to the circus.

Rᴇᴠɪꜱɪᴏɴ: _____

_____

_____

2 This is a story about the time I was chased by a ghost in a haunted house.

Rᴇᴠɪꜱɪᴏɴ: _____

_____

_____

3 I will tell you about my rock-climbing adventure on Mount Sherman.

Rᴇᴠɪꜱɪᴏɴ: _____

_____

_____

4 Once upon a time, I got a new dog.

Rᴇᴠɪꜱɪᴏɴ: _____

_____

_____

Getting Started

When we read effective writing, the words flow in such a way that they almost disappear into the meaning, purpose, and voice of the piece. This kind of fluency is no accident; the writing is constructed with this objective in mind. Student writers often get stuck in two traps that restrict the fluency of their pieces:

THE GROCERY LIST

Rather than describing each detail in a separate, well-constructed sentence, the author simply lists all the attributes in a single sentence.

> EXAMPLE: *The old dog was brown, scruffy, dirty, mean, slow, and snarly.*

THE BROKEN RECORD (or, nowadays, the broken CD?)

Each sentence begins in the same way, which results in monotony.

> EXAMPLE: *He had long black hair. He had a striped shirt. He had dark, bushy eyebrows.*
> *He had a bandana tied around his head. He had a big, gold earring in his ear and*
> *a sword in his hand.*

It is important for students to recognize these common pitfalls and learn strategies to overcome them. The activities in this section teach students how to:

1 Separate the grocery list by giving each detail its own descriptive sentence.

2 Replace repetitive pronouns with more interesting alternatives. (Replace *he* with *the fellow, man, chap, giant,* and so on.)

3 Achieve sentence variety by using a different subject. (Instead of *He wore a red coat,* use *A red coat hugged his frame.*)

4 Achieve sentence variety by beginning sentences with *-ing* verbs (participles) rather than subjects. (*Looking over his shoulder, he began to run.*)

Before introducing the activity sheets, discuss the concepts and objectives first. There are several activity sheets of each type—you might model one sheet for the class and use another as a whole-class activity. You can use the remaining sheets for independent work.

Name _____   Date _____

Separating the Grocery List–1

 **Writer's Tip:** Description is what brings a story to life. When you are describing something important, be sure to give each detail its own sentence to help readers see it in their minds.

DIRECTIONS: Although the description below includes some interesting details, it is still a grocery list! Underline the items in the list and write a separate, well-constructed sentence for each.

> The zoo was exciting! We saw an elephant raising his trunk, a giraffe strolling across a field, a polar bear taking a nap, and several seals swimming gracefully.

REVISION: _____

_____

_____

_____

_____

_____

_____

_____

_____

_____

_____

Super Story-Writing Strategies & Activities Scholastic Professional Books

Name_____ Date_____

Separating the Grocery List–2

Writer's Tip: Description is what brings a story to life. When you are describing something important, be sure to give each detail its own sentence to help readers see it in their minds.

DIRECTIONS: Although the description below includes some interesting details, it is still a grocery list! Underline the items in the list, and write a separate, well-constructed sentence for each.

The kitchen was a mess! There were tomatoes on the floor, noodles all over the counter, pureed carrots splattered on the wall, and pudding smeared on the ceiling.

REVISION:_____

_____

_____

_____

_____

_____

_____

_____

_____

_____

_____

_____

Name _____   Date _____

Separating the Grocery List–3

Writer's Tip: Description is what brings a story to life. When you are describing something important, be sure to give each detail its own sentence to help readers see it in their minds.

DIRECTIONS: Read each sentence. Then revise it so that each detail has its own separate, well-constructed sentence.

EXAMPLE: *It was a bright, sunny, hot summer day.*

REVISION: *I shielded my eyes from the bright afternoon sunshine. There was not a cloud in the sky, and the sun burned stronger than ever. I wiped the sweat from my forehead as I looked for a shady spot to rest.*

Now it's your turn. How would you separate these grocery lists?

1 It was a bright, sunny, hot summer day.

REVISION: _____

_____

_____

_____

2 The woods were dark, damp, and mysterious.

REVISION: _____

_____

_____

_____

Super Story-Writing Strategies & Activities Scholastic Professional Books

Name _____ Date _____

Separating the Grocery List–4

Writer's Tip: Description is what brings a story to life. When you are describing something important, be sure to give each detail its own sentence to help readers see it in their minds.

DIRECTIONS: Read each sentence. Then revise it so that each detail has its own separate, well-constructed sentence.

> EXAMPLE: *In the room, there were dirty clothes, piles of newspapers, and old food.*

> REVISION: *I looked around the room. Dirty clothes were tossed over the bed and piled on chairs. Newspapers were stacked knee-high, leaving only a narrow pathway. A terrible smell of old, rotting food hung in the air.*

Now it's your turn. How would you separate these grocery lists?

1 **In the room, there were dirty clothes, newspapers, and old food.**

REVISION: _____

_____

_____

_____

2 **The beautiful meadow was filled with flowers, trees, and birds.**

REVISION: _____

_____

_____

_____

Name _____ Date _____

Separating the Grocery List–5

 **Writer's Tip:** Description is what brings a story to life. When you are describing something important, be sure to give each detail its own sentence to help readers see it in their minds.

DIRECTIONS: Read each sentence. Then revise it so that each detail has its own separate, well-constructed sentence.

EXAMPLE: *The dog had fluffy brown fur, big eyes, long ears, and a wagging tail.*

REVISION: *Soft, fluffy fur that was a beautiful shade of chocolate brown covered the dog's large body. His big, gentle brown eyes kept a careful watch. As he bounded around the yard, his floppy ears swung in the breeze. His long, sleek tail told a happy story.*

Now it's your turn. How would you separate these grocery lists?

1 **The dog had fluffy brown fur, big eyes, long ears, and a wagging tail.**

REVISION: _____

_____

_____

_____

2 **The stranger had a pale complexion, dark hair, and fearful eyes.**

REVISION: _____

_____

_____

_____

18

Name _____ Date _____

Fixing the Broken Record–1

 **Writer's Tip:** In order for your writing to be interesting, you must use sentence variety. That means that each sentence should begin a bit differently.

DIRECTIONS: Read the passage below and underline the parts that repeat.

> *He was so tall that he actually towered over a nearby pine tree. He was wearing a pair of tattered overalls that hung from his lean frame. He was carrying a fishing pole and a garbage can. I stepped closer to get a better look.*

Think of several other ways that you could refer to the man in this passage. Here are some examples:

> *The mysterious giant*
> *The enormous man*
> *The extraordinary creature*

Now replace the word *he* with a more interesting choice. Fill in the blanks below.

_____ was so tall that he actually towered over a nearby pine tree. He was wearing a pair of tattered overalls that hung from his lean frame.

_____ was carrying a fishing pole and a garbage can. I stepped closer to get a better look.

Now look at another description of the giant.

> He was so tall that his head appeared to be in the clouds. He was wearing blue jeans and a flannel shirt that were too small for him. He was carrying a long rope that dangled behind him. I stepped closer to get a better look.

_____ was so tall that his head appeared to be in the clouds. He was wearing blue jeans and a flannel shirt that were too small for him.

_____ was carrying a long rope that dangled behind him. I stepped closer to get a better look.

Name _____   Date _____

Fixing the Broken Record–2

Writer's Tip: In order for your writing to be interesting, you must use sentence variety. That means that each sentence should begin a bit differently.

DIRECTIONS: Read the passage below and underline the parts that repeat.

She had long, straight hair the color of a crow. She had pearly white skin that seemed to shimmer. She had a long tail covered with glittering blue and green scales.

Think of several other ways that you could refer to the mermaid. Here are some examples:

The unusual woman
The lovely lady
The beautiful creature
The strange being
The mysterious mermaid

Now replace the word *she* with a more interesting choice. Fill in the blanks below.

_____ had long, straight hair the color of a crow. She had pearly white skin that seemed to shimmer.

_____ had a long tail covered with glittering blue and green scales.

Now look at another description of the mermaid.

She had long, braided hair carefully entwined with ribbons of seaweed. She had golden, sun-kissed skin splashed with sparkling drops of water. She had a long, scaly green tail that gently flipped up and down.

_____ had long, braided hair carefully entwined with ribbons of seaweed. She had golden, sun-kissed skin splashed with sparkling drops of water. _____ had a long, scaly green tail that gently flipped up and down.

BONUS QUESTION: Why do you think you wouldn't replace every single *she* in this example? What do *you* think the mermaid looks like? Use the sentence starters above to help. On another sheet of paper, write three sentences describing the mermaid's hair, skin, and tail.

Super Story-Writing Strategies & Activities Scholastic Professional Books

Name_____ Date _____

Fixing the Broken Record–3

 **Writer's Tip:** In order for your writing to be interesting, you must use sentence variety. That means that each sentence should begin a bit differently.

DIRECTIONS: Read the passage below and underline the parts that repeat.

> *He looked over his shoulder and began to run. He pumped hard with his arms and pounded the pavement with his feet. He dragged his bag of stolen goods behind him and sprinted out of sight.*

One way to have sentence variety is to begin some sentences with an *-ing* verb instead of the subject. Look at the differences between these pairs of sentences.

> *He looked over his shoulder and began to run.*
> *Looking over his shoulder, he began to run.*

> *He dragged his bag of stolen goods behind him and sprinted out of sight.*
> *Dragging his bag of stolen goods behind him, he sprinted out of sight.*

Notice how the second sentences start with a verb instead of "He…" Revise the following sentences in the same way. The first two have been started for you.

1 **The skater glided across the ice and smiled at the audience.**
REVISION:
Gliding across the ice, the skater _____

2 **The movie star looked glamorous and waved at the fans.**
REVISION:
Looking _____, the movie star _____

3 **Harry hurried to school and fell on a patch of ice.**
REVISION:
Hurrying _____

4 **The frog leapt from lily pad to lily pad and crossed the pond.**
REVISION:
Leaping _____

Name _____   Date _____

Changing the Subject–1

 **Writer's Tip:** In order for your writing to be interesting, you must use sentence variety. That means that each sentence should begin a bit differently.

DIRECTIONS: Revise each sentence so that it does not begin with "He...." Instead of always beginning a sentence with the subject, start with the object. Be sure to add some interesting adjectives and verbs.

EXAMPLE: *He had straggly hair.*

REVISION: *Long, dark, straggly hair framed the stranger's face.*

1 **He wore a long black cape.**

REVISION: _____

_____

2 **He had a big hat.**

REVISION: _____

_____

3 **He carried a parakeet on his shoulder.**

REVISION: _____

_____

4 **He had a sneering expression on his face.**

REVISION: _____

_____

Name_____ Date_____

Changing the Subject-2

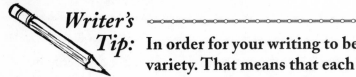

Writer's Tip: In order for your writing to be interesting, you must use sentence variety. That means that each sentence should begin a bit differently.

DIRECTIONS: Revise each sentence so that it does not begin with "She...." Instead of always beginning a sentence with the subject, start with the object. Be sure to add some interesting adjectives and verbs.

EXAMPLE: *She had long black hair.*

REVISION: *Long, shiny black hair cascaded over her shoulders.*

1 **She had brown eyes.**

REVISION: _____

_____

2 **She wore a purple shawl.**

REVISION: _____

_____

3 **She had leather boots.**

REVISION: _____

_____

4 **She carried a pink handbag the size of a small suitcase.**

REVISION: _____

_____

Name _____   Date _____

Changing the Subject–3

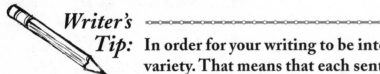

Writer's Tip: In order for your writing to be interesting, you must use sentence variety. That means that each sentence should begin a bit differently.

DIRECTIONS: Revise each sentence so that it does not begin with "There was…" or "There were…." Be sure to add some interesting adjectives and verbs.

EXAMPLE: *There was a chair in the corner of the room.*

REVISION: *A fluffy, soft chair sat nestled in the corner of the room.*

1 There were lace curtains on the windows.

REVISION: _____

_____

2 There was a green carpet on the floor.

REVISION: _____

_____

3 There were books on the shelves.

REVISION: _____

_____

4 There was a mysterious portrait hanging in the corner.

REVISION: _____

_____

Name _____ Date _____

Changing the Subject—4

Writer's Tip: In order for your writing to be interesting, you must use sentence variety. That means that each sentence should begin a bit differently.

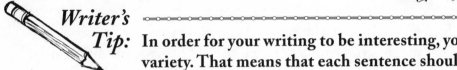

DIRECTIONS: Revise each sentence so that it does not begin with "There was..." or "There were...." Be sure to add some interesting adjectives and verbs.

EXAMPLE: *There were tall trees in the back of the yard.*

REVISION: *Tall trees stood across the back of the yard like soldiers.*

1 **There were bushes along the side of the house.**

REVISION: _____

_____

2 **There was a fence around the yard.**

REVISION: _____

_____

3 **There were flowers in the garden.**

REVISION: _____

_____

4 **There were butterflies everywhere.**

REVISION: _____

_____

Name _____ Date _____

Changing the Subject–5

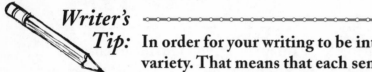

Writer's Tip: In order for your writing to be interesting, you must use sentence variety. That means that each sentence should begin a bit differently.

DIRECTIONS: Revise each sentence so that it does not begin with "I saw..." or "I liked...." Instead of always beginning a sentence with the subject, start with the object. Be sure to add some interesting adjectives and verbs.

EXAMPLE: *I saw a treasure chest in the corner of the attic.*

REVISION: *An old wooden treasure chest sat undisturbed in the darkest corner of the attic.*

1 **I saw cobwebs on the treasure chest.**

REVISION: _____

_____

2 **I saw a broken lock on the treasure chest.**

REVISION: _____

_____

3 **I liked the jewels in the treasure chest.**

REVISION: _____

_____

4 **I liked the mysterious map we found at the bottom of the treasure chest.**

REVISION: _____

_____

Super Story-Writing Strategies & Activities Scholastic Professional Books

Getting Started

Elaborative detail is what brings a piece of writing to life. Using specific rather than general adjectives can help. For example: *The blue chiffon dress hung by the door* is better than *The pretty dress hung by the door*. *The sleek red sports car* is more effective than *The cool car*. These small brushstrokes of specificity can drastically improve a piece of writing.

When deciding what to describe in a story, an author must determine which characters, settings, and objects are story-critical. Story-critical characters, settings, and objects affect the main character and the outcome of the story. They are critical to the plot. Once an author decides what to describe, he or she often uses the five senses to draw the reader into the story and bring story-critical characters, settings, and objects to life!

To write detailed, effective description, authors can begin by asking questions about the story-critical setting, character, or object they wish to describe. They may ask questions about:

- color
- size
- texture
- shape
- material
- age
- condition
- smell
- sound
- what it reminds you of
- physical features (eyes, nose, mouth, ears, hair, stature, build)

EXAMPLE:
Ask children to describe an old box you found in the attic. They should imagine what it looks like. (They may wish to draw it first.) Then ask them relevant questions about the box, such as:

- How big is it?

- What is it made out of?
- What color is it?
- Is it smooth or rough?
- How old is it?
- Whom did it belong to?
- What was it used for?

Translate the answers into sentences to create an interesting description.

EXAMPLE:
The old dusty box sat in the corner. Its wooden sides were splintered along the bottom and a worn coat of faded blue paint was still visible across the top. It was roughly the size and shape of a large suitcase. As I ran my hand along its lid, I was surprised at the smooth, cool feel of the wood. I decided that someone long ago must have taken very good care of the box, and perhaps had stored something special inside.

Note the sentence variety in the above passage. It is not a "grocery list." (*It was smooth, blue, wooden, and old.*) Nor is it a "broken record." (*It was wooden. It was old. It was blue. It was smooth.*) Each sentence begins in a slightly different way. The description allows readers to see the old box in their "mind's eye."

Each activity sheet in this section of the book presents students with a general description of a character, setting, or object. Help them generate sensory questions (not yes or no questions such as "Is it big?"). Then show them how to use their answers to create dazzling descriptions. Encourage them to write one specific detail in each of the four or five sentences. It is helpful to discuss this concept first and model examples for students before they begin.

NOTE: The Sensory Sentence-Starter Chart on page 33 is for use with the activities on pages 34–37. It is helpful to make a copy for each student.

Name_____ Date_____

Paint a Picture–1

 **Writer's Tip:** General adjectives, such as *good*, *cool*, *great*, *nice*, and *pretty*, do not give the reader a clear picture of what they describe. Instead, authors use specific descriptive words to "paint a picture."

DIRECTIONS: Read the general description below. Write three or four sentences that paint a picture of the underlined word. (The description has been started for you.) Be sure to use the five senses!

> EXAMPLE: *It was an old <u>fence</u>.* (Ask yourself what the fence looked like. What other senses can you incorporate into your description?)

> REVISION: *As I stood in front of the house, I looked around. The fence, with its missing pickets, barely wrapped itself around the old yard. Its once bright white color could be seen here and there peeking through the gray peeling paint. The gate hung loosely from the rusted hinges and squeaked as it waved in the breeze.*

Which of the five senses is left out of this description, and why?

_____

Now it's your turn. How can you paint a picture of the underlined word?

The unique <u>crystal</u> must have been magical.

REVISION: **I gazed into the crystal in the palm of my hand.** _____

_____

_____

_____

_____

_____

_____

_____

28

Name _____   Date _____

Paint a Picture–2

 **Writer's Tip:** General adjectives, such as *good*, *cool*, *great*, *nice*, and *pretty*, do not give the reader a clear picture of what they describe. Instead, authors use specific descriptive words to "paint a picture."

DIRECTIONS: Read the general description below. Write three or four sentences that paint a picture of the underlined word. (The description has been started for you.) Be sure to use the five senses!

> EXAMPLE: *My <u>bedroom</u> was messy.* (Ask yourself what you might see, feel, smell, or hear in your messy room.)

> REVISION: *I looked around my messy room. Dirty clothes were thrown on the floor. Potato chips crunched beneath my feet. My bed was covered with papers and school assignments. I wrinkled my nose at the smell of sour milk on the bedside table.*

Now it's your turn. How can you paint a picture of the underlined word?

The <u>forest</u> was spooky.

REVISION: **I couldn't believe the spooky scene before me.** _____

_____

_____

_____

_____

_____

_____

_____

_____

Name _____   Date _____

Paint a Picture-3

Writer's Tip: General adjectives, such as *good*, *cool*, *great*, *nice*, and *pretty*, do not give the reader a clear picture of what they describe. Instead, authors use specific descriptive words to "paint a picture."

DIRECTIONS: Read the general description below. Write three or four sentences that paint a picture of the underlined word. (The description has been started for you.) Be sure to use the five senses!

EXAMPLE: *The <u>meadow</u> was pretty.* (Ask yourself what you might see, feel, smell, or hear in the meadow.)

REVISION: *I stood in the middle of the meadow. Tall, graceful grass blew gently in the breeze. The scent of wildflowers filled the air, and butterflies flitted from flower to flower. I closed my eyes and listened to the wind rustling the grass and birds calling overhead.*

Now it's your turn. How can you paint a picture of the underlined word?

The <u>beach</u> was nice.

REVISION: **The smooth, white, sandy beach stretched out before me.**

_____

_____

_____

_____

_____

_____

_____

Name _____ Date _____

Paint a Picture-4

 **Writer's Tip:** General adjectives, such as *good, cool, great, nice,* and *pretty,* do not give the reader a clear picture of what they describe. Instead, authors use specific descriptive words to "paint a picture."

DIRECTIONS: Read the general description. Write three or four sentences that paint a picture of the underlined word. (The description has been started for you.) Be sure to use the five senses!

EXAMPLE: *The <u>witch</u> looked mean!* (Ask yourself questions about her physical features and clothing.)

REVISION: *There I was, face to face with a witch! Her beady, black eyes stared out at me from beneath her pointed hat. A long, tattered black dress hung over her tall, thin frame and nearly covered her red-and-white stockings peeking out from below the hem. I tried not to stare at her long, hooked nose with a dark, bulbous wart on the end. Her sneering mouth let out a cackle that sent shivers up my spine!*

Now it's your turn. How can you paint a picture of the underlined word?

The <u>princess</u> was beautiful.

REVISION: I was shocked to find myself standing before the princess!

_____

_____

_____

_____

_____

_____

_____

Name _____ Date _____

Paint a Picture-5

 **Writer's Tip:** General adjectives, such as *good*, *cool*, *great*, *nice*, and *pretty*, do not give the reader a clear picture of what they describe. Instead, authors use specific descriptive words to "paint a picture."

DIRECTIONS: Read the general description. Write three or four sentences that paint a picture of the underlined word. (The description has been started for you.) Be sure to use the five senses!

EXAMPLE: *The <u>sword</u> was awesome.* (Ask yourself what the sword was made out of and how it was decorated.)

REVISION: *I held the sword in my hands and gasped at its magnificence. It was extremely heavy and probably cast in solid gold. The edges gleamed in the sunlight and glinted as I tipped it this way and that. The handle was embedded with all kinds of gemstones—rubies, emeralds, sapphires, and many others. I raised it high and noticed a large oval diamond beneath the handle. That's when I knew the sword must have belonged to a famous knight or perhaps even a king!*

Now it's your turn. How can you paint a picture of the underlined word?

The <u>crown</u> was fancy.

REVISION: **I stared at the amazing crown.** _____

_____

_____

_____

_____

_____

_____

_____

Name _____ Date _____

Sensory Sentence-Starter Chart

Writer's Tip: To create a vivid description, writers use the five senses. They also vary their sentence structure so that their writing flows and does not sound repetitive.

Sensory Sentence-Starter Chart

What you see
I gazed…
Looking carefully, I noticed…
I was surprised to see…
I peered at…
I couldn't help but notice …

What you hear
Standing quietly, I noticed…
I could make out the sound of…
I listened closely to…
I strained to hear…

What you feel
I felt…
When I ran my hand along it, I…
I enjoyed the feel of the…
When I touched …

What you smell
Breathing deeply, I noticed…
I sniffed at…
The aroma of…
I inhaled the scent of…

What you taste
My mouth watered as…
I smacked my lips as…
My stomach growled as…
I tasted…

Name _____   Date _____

Sensory Sentence-Starters–1

Writer's Tip: To create a vivid description, writers use the five senses. They also vary their sentence structure so that their writing flows and does not sound repetitive.

DIRECTIONS: The paragraph below provides a vivid description, but it does not display sentence variety. Above each bold-faced phrase, write an appropriate alternative from the Sensory Sentence-Starter Chart (page 33). You may need to revise each sentence so that it makes sense with its new beginning.

I paused on the forest path and looked around. **I saw** hundreds of tall

trees reaching for the sky. **I heard** the sounds of birds chirping as they

flitted from tree to tree. **There were** small wildflowers of every

imaginable color. **There were** butterflies fluttering around each blossom.

I saw a mother deer and her spotted fawn darting between the trees.

There was the green, mossy smell of the forest floor. **There was** a spongy

feeling of a hundred year's worth of pine needles underfoot.

Name _____   Date _____

Sensory Sentence-Starters—2

Writer's Tip: To create a vivid description, writers use the five senses. They also vary their sentence structure so that their writing flows and does not sound repetitive.

DIRECTIONS: The paragraph below provides a vivid description, but it does not display sentence variety. Above each bold-faced phrase, write an appropriate alternative from the Sensory Sentence-Starter Chart (page 33). You may need to revise each sentence so that it makes sense with its new beginning.

The autumn landscape was beautiful! **I saw** trees with leaves of blazing

red, gold, and orange. **I heard** the sounds of geese honking overhead as

they began their flight south. **There were** bright orange pumpkins and

tall cornstalks dotting the fields. **There were** dry leaves beneath my feet

that crackled as I walked. **I saw** a bright blue sky sprinkled with puffy

white clouds. **There was** the smell of freshly baked apple pie coming

from a nearby window. **There was** a cool, brisk breeze blowing through

my hair.

Name _____ Date _____

Use Your Senses–1

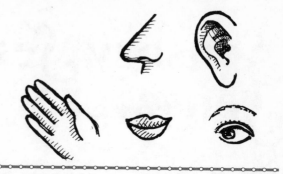

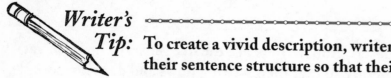
Writer's Tip: To create a vivid description, writers use the five senses. They also vary their sentence structure so that their writing flows and does not sound repetitive.

DIRECTIONS: Read the sentence below and answer the questions to brainstorm details.

The city was certainly a busy place!

What did you see? _____

What did you hear? _____

What did you feel (touch)? _____

What did you smell? _____

What did you taste? _____

Now use your answers to write a paragraph about the city. Don't forget to vary your sentence beginnings by using the Sensory Sentence-Starter Chart (page 33).

_____

_____

_____

_____

_____

_____

_____

_____

_____

Super Story-Writing Strategies & Activities Scholastic Professional Books

Name _____ Date _____

Use Your Senses-2

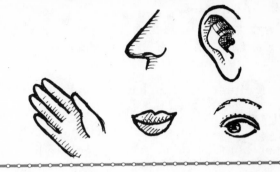

 **Writer's Tip:** To create a vivid description, writers use the five senses. They also vary their sentence structure so that their writing flows and does not sound repetitive.

DIRECTIONS: Read the sentence below and answer the questions to brainstorm details.

The baseball stadium was filled to capacity!

What did you see? _____

What did you hear? _____

What did you feel (touch)? _____

What did you smell? _____

What did you taste? _____

Now use your answers to write a paragraph about the stadium. Don't forget to vary your sentence beginnings by using the Sensory Sentence-Starter Chart (page 33).

_____

_____

_____

_____

_____

_____

_____

_____

_____

Getting Started

Students often have a good idea of the direction their stories will take, but they find it difficult to link story sections effectively. After writing a detailed description of a character, object, or setting, they might find it difficult to make a transition back to the plot. Some students even struggle to link one action to the next, falling into a series of *and then*'s.

EXAMPLE: *I went outside and then I saw the fairy. Then I went into the forest with the fairy. And then I saw the other fairies. There were lots and lots of them. And then they did a fairy dance. Then I joined them.*

One way to help students move their stories along is to provide them with a number of transitional words and phrases that can be used instead of the usual *then* or *next*. We refer to these as "red flags." These phrases alert the reader that there is a story shift or a twist in the plot, such as a significant event or a surprising discovery. Sometimes a single word, such as *suddenly,* can be used as a red flag. Display the following chart:

> ### Red Flags
>
> *A moment later…*
> *Before I knew it …*
> *In the blink of an eye…*
> *All of a sudden…*
> *Just as I realized…*
> *The next thing I knew…*
> *Just then…*
> *After that …*
> *Suddenly…*

The activity sheets in this section provide students with opportunities to experiment with a variety of red flags that will help them move their stories along. Introduce this section by displaying your chart of red flags and reading aloud the example provided above. As a class, substitute all the repetitive *and then*'s with alternate phrases.

Encourage children to be on the lookout for red flags as they read on their own. Throughout the year, they can add these new phrases to the chart. Whenever students get stuck in their writing, they can refer to the chart for a number of options to get them moving right along!

Name _____ Date _____

Red Flag Menu

Writer's Tip: One way an author can get the reader's attention is by using phrases that we call "red flags." Red flags, such as *all of a sudden* or *the next thing I knew*, indicate a new twist in the plot. Red flags can replace predictable words and phrases, like *next* or *and then*.

DIRECTIONS: Read the sample sentences below. Then create your own "Red Flag Menu" by filling in the blanks with as many red flags as you can think of. The menu has been started for you.

MY RED FLAG MENU

_____Suddenly_____	I managed to escape from the monster.
_____Just then_____	I managed to escape from the monster.
____A moment later____	I managed to escape from the monster.
_____	I managed to escape from the monster.
_____	I managed to escape from the monster.
_____	I managed to escape from the monster.
_____	I managed to escape from the monster.
_____	I managed to escape from the monster.
_____	I managed to escape from the monster.
_____	I managed to escape from the monster.
_____	I managed to escape from the monster.
_____	I managed to escape from the monster.
_____	I managed to escape from the monster.
_____	I managed to escape from the monster.

Name _____   Date _____

Warning! Red Flags–1

Writer's Tip: One way an author can get the reader's attention is by using phrases that we call "red flags." Red flags, such as *all of a sudden* or *the next thing I knew*, indicate a new twist in the plot. Red flags can replace predictable words and phrases, like *next* or *and then*.

Directions: Read the story below. Each time the words *and then* appear, replace them with a better red flag.

Pulling my sled behind me, I trudged through the snowy mountain pass. The sky grew darker by the minute and the frosty wind began to blow. **And then** it began to snow. The snow came down heavily and the wind blew in my face. **And then** I saw something approaching. It was impossible to tell what it was, but it cast a long shadow on the ground. As it got closer, I realized it was a snow monster! It was the size of a pine tree and was covered in dirty, ice-crusted white fur. The beast had long fangs and curved, black claws. **And then** it started coming toward me. I began to tremble with fright, but I knew I had to do something. **And then** I turned around and began to run. **And then** I got an idea. I crossed my fingers, hoping my plan would work. **And then** I ran to the edge of the hill and jumped on my sled. **And then** I zoomed off down the hill, leaving the snow monster far behind me!

Here are a few red flags to get you started:

> *Just then*
> *In the blink of an eye*
> *Before I knew it*
> *A second later*

Name _____ Date _____

Warning! Red Flags-2

Writer's Tip: One way an author can get the reader's attention is by using phrases that we call "red flags." Red flags, such as *all of a sudden* or *the next thing I knew*, indicate a new twist in the plot. Red flags can replace predictable words and phrases, like *next* or *and then*.

DIRECTIONS: Read the story below. Each time the word *next* appears, replace it with a better red flag.

Would I ever get past the sleeping skeleton guarding the cave? I had to get inside somehow and capture the treasure! I tiptoed closer. **Next**, the skeleton stirred. I stopped, holding my breath, and then crept on. **Next**, the skeleton sat upright and stared out into the night. **Next**, I dropped to the ground and crawled forward, hoping the skeleton wouldn't see me. **Next**, there was a swishing sound above me. I raised my head and sneaked a peak. The skeleton was standing over me, swinging his sword over my head. **Next**, I threw myself forward and grabbed hold of his bony legs. **Next**, he toppled to the ground, falling into a big pile of bones. **Next**, I got up and ran past the bone pile and into the cave to capture the treasure!

Super Story-Writing Strategies & Activities Scholastic Professional Books

Name _____ Date _____

Warning! Red Flags–3

Writer's Tip: One way an author can get the reader's attention is by using phrases that we call "red flags." Red flags, such as *all of a sudden* or *the next thing I knew*, indicate a new twist in the plot. Red flags can replace predictable words and phrases, like *next* or *and then*.

DIRECTIONS: Find at least three places in the story below where red flags would be effective. Underline each place and write a word or phrase above it.

I looked off in the distance. I noticed the horizon was getting darker as large, threatening gray clouds gathered and rolled in my direction. The storm still looks pretty far away, I thought as I climbed into my small boat. I started the engine and headed home. An unusually cold breeze sliced through the hot air. I looked back and saw that the storm was moving much faster than I had anticipated. The waves were crashing over the edge of the boat. I cranked up the speed. I heard a large clap of thunder. Almost at the same time, the rain came pouring down on my head and into my boat. Oh, no! I thought as my little boat tossed around like a toy in the tub. I strained to see as water splashed in my eyes. I saw it! The shore was in sight. Bang! Another clap of thunder sounded as I moved closer to safety. I aimed the boat toward the shore and fought the waves to get there. I was safely on land.

Super Story-Writing Strategies & Activities Scholastic Professional Books

Getting Started

A successful short story opens with an interesting beginning that immediately draws the reader in. The author might spend a bit of time describing the setting, introducing the character(s), and establishing the purpose for the action. All of this should build up to a single, meaningful main event. In short, the main event is what the story is all about. The main event consists of the adventure, problem, or experience that changes the main character in some way.

Because of the importance of the main event, this portion of the story should take up more space relative to the other story elements. It should be longer than the beginning, the description of the setting, the solution, or the ending. Instead, children often rush through the main event by summarizing it in one or two very general sentences.

EXAMPLE: *The ghost chased me, but I got away.*

This event would be much more exciting if the author included one or more of the following:

◉ A play-by-play account of the action (the chase in slow motion)

◉ A detailed description of a story-critical setting, character, or object (the ghost)

◉ An exclamation a character might make (What would the main character or ghost say?)

◉ The main character's thoughts and feelings about the event (how she felt during the chase)

Watch what happens to the above summary when the author elaborates on the main event with slow-motion action, description, thoughts, feelings, and exclamations.

The ghost was right behind me. I could feel the filmy mist that surrounded him settling on my shoulders. I shivered and concentrated on running as fast as I could. Glancing behind me, I saw the tall, wispy phantom grinning maliciously and floating toward me like a fog. I took a deep breath and shouted, "Get away from me, you ghoul!" The ghost cackled and I felt a clammy moisture seep into my shirt. My knees felt weak and my heart pounded, but somehow I kept running instinctively toward the light at the top of the stairs. That was when the ghoul began to slow down, and I realized that he would never step into the light. He faded back into the darkness of the basement, and I knew I was safe.

Students can begin to elaborate on their own writing by asking themselves questions, such as:

◉ What did you do? (in slow motion!)

◉ What did you observe? (using the five senses)

◉ What did you think or feel? (emotionally and physically)

◉ What did you say?

The activities in this section are designed to raise these questions and draw out the kind of elaboration that will turn summarized action into fully described main events!

Name _____ Date _____

Builders and Stretchers–1

Writer's Tip: When you get to the most important part of your story, don't just summarize it! Build it up and stretch it out with action, description, exclamation, thoughts, and feelings.

DIRECTIONS: Read the summary of the important event below, and answer the questions that follow.

   A lion chased me through the jungle.

Think of the sentence in parts:

   A lion   chased me   through the jungle.

A lion
As you glanced over your shoulder, what did the lion look like?

_____

_____

chased me
What might you have exclaimed as you were being chased?

_____

_____

How did you feel while you were being chased?

_____

_____

through the jungle
What did the jungle look like? Describe the sounds, smells, and sights around you.

_____

_____

Notice how much stronger your main event is when you read all of your answers together!

Super Story-Writing Strategies & Activities Scholastic Professional Books

Name _____ Date _____

Builders and Stretchers–2

Writer's Tip: When you get to the most important part of your story, don't just summarize it! Build it up and stretch it out with action, description, exclamation, thoughts, and feelings.

DIRECTIONS: Read the summary of the important event below, and then answer the questions that follow.

I explored an old, abandoned house and met a ghost.

Think of the sentence in parts:

I explored   *an old, abandoned house*   *and met a ghost.*

I explored
Describe how you moved through the house. How did you feel?

_____

_____

an old, abandoned house
What did the house look like? Write two or three descriptive sentences.

_____

_____

and met a ghost
In two or three sentences, describe what the ghost looked like.

_____

_____

What did you exclaim when you met the ghost?

_____

_____

Notice how much stronger your main event is when you read all of your answers together!

Name _____ Date _____

Builders and Stretchers–3

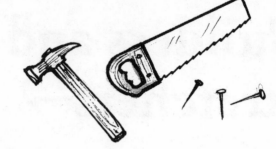

 **Writer's Tip:** When you get to the most important part of your story, don't just summarize it! Build it up and stretch it out with action, description, exclamation, thoughts, and feelings.

DIRECTIONS: Read the summary of the important event below, and answer the questions that follow.

A space creature took me for a ride.

Think of the sentence in parts:

A space creature   took me   for a ride.

A space creature
When you opened the door, what did you see? What did the creature look like?

_____

_____

took me
How did you feel as you looked at the creature? What did you exclaim?

_____

_____

for a ride
What kind of ride was it?

_____

How did you feel during the ride?

_____

What did you see while you were on the ride?

_____

Notice how much stronger your main event is when you read all of your answers together!

Super Story-Writing Strategies & Activities Scholastic Professional Books

Name _____ Date _____

Builders and Stretchers—4

Writer's Tip: When you get to the most important part of your story, don't just summarize it! Build it up and stretch it out with action, description, exclamation, thoughts, and feelings.

DIRECTIONS: Read the summary of the important event below, and answer the questions that follow.

A dolphin took me for a swim in the ocean.

Think of the sentence in parts:

A dolphin   took me for a swim   in the ocean.

A dolphin
How did the dolphin look and what did it feel like?

_____

_____

took me for a swim
What did you exclaim as you headed into the ocean?

_____

_____

How did it feel to swim with the dolphin?

_____

_____

in the ocean
Describe the scene in the ocean by using the five senses.

_____

_____

Notice how much stronger your main event is when you read all of your answers together!

Name _____   Date _____

Builders and Stretchers–5

Writer's Tip: When you get to the most important part of your story, don't just summarize it! Build it up and stretch it out with action, description, exclamation, thoughts, and feelings.

DIRECTIONS: Read the summary of the important event below, and answer the questions that follow.

> *My pet monkey escaped from her cage and ran through the house.*

Think of the sentence in parts:

> *My pet monkey*   *escaped from her cage*   *and ran through the house.*

My pet monkey
What did the monkey look like?

_____

_____

escaped from her cage
What did you exclaim when you noticed she was missing?

_____

How did you feel when you saw that she had escaped?

_____

_____

and ran through the house
What was the monkey doing as she ran through the house?

_____

What did the house look like while and after the monkey ran through it?

_____

Notice how much stronger your main event is when you read all of your answers together!

Super Story-Writing Strategies & Activities Scholastic Professional Books

Getting Started

A common pitfall in student writing is the tendency for some children to write an ongoing stream of dialogue. We call this "wiretap" writing because it sounds exactly like an overheard conversation. Wiretap writing can be either an external conversation or an internal conversation. For example:

"Hi, Tom."
"Hi."
"Want to explore that old haunted house?"
"Yeah."
"Cool."
"Let's go."
(This is an external conversation.)

I think I'll go explore the haunted house in the woods. Okay, here I am outside of the house. Wow, it sure looks scary, but I think I'll go in anyway. Oh boy! What was that noise?
(This is an internal conversation.)

In either case, it is not enough just to tell students to avoid this kind of writing. Students need to see and feel the difference between "wiretap" writing and a balance of dialogue, action, and description. Show them how they can convert "all talk" into action and description in order to achieve a better balance.

Write this example on the board:

All Talk	Action	Description
"Hi, Tom." *"Hi."*	*We said hello.*	
"That is such a cute kitten."		*The kitten was a small ball of soft, orange-striped fur. Her bright blue eyes seemed to twinkle and she shifted her tiny pointed ears this way and that.*

Then have students write a few sentences of action or description to replace the talk in these two examples.

All Talk	Action	Description
"Let's go to the mall." *"Okay."*		
"That cellar is scary! I wish I didn't have to go down there."		

Now your students will be ready to do the activity sheets in this section. Start by completing one activity as directed practice with the whole class, and then assign other activities for independent practice.

Name _____   Date _____

Too Much Talk–1

Writer's Tip: Remember that stories with all talk (no action or description) are hard for the reader to follow. Instead, use a balance of dialogue, action, and description.

DIRECTIONS: Read the dialogue below. Then change it to action or description.

> **EXAMPLE:** *"It's a great day for sledding."*
> *"You're right!"*
> *"Let's bring our sleds to Academy Hill!"*
> *"Great idea! Let's go!"*

> **REVISION:** (dialogue changed to action)
> *We decided that it was a great day for sledding and set off for Academy Hill.*

1 Change this dialogue into action (1 sentence):

> **"Let's go camping."**
> **"Okay. Let's get our stuff."**
> **"Do you have everything?"**
> **"Yes."**
> **"Then let's go!"**

_____

_____

_____

2 Change this dialogue into a description (2–3 sentences):

> **"That bear is huge!"**
> **"It looks really mean!"**
> **"It's got big claws and teeth!"**
> **"I'm really scared!"**

_____

_____

_____

Super Story-Writing Strategies & Activities Scholastic Professional Books

Name _____ Date _____

Too Much Talk-2

Writer's Tip: Remember that stories with all talk (no action or description) are hard for the reader to follow. Instead, use a balance of dialogue, action, and description.

DIRECTIONS: Read the dialogue below. Then change it to action or description.

EXAMPLE: *"Wow! What an awesome room!"*
"I'd love a bedroom like that!"
"It's got everything you could want!

REVISION: (dialogue changed to description) *The room was small and cozy with shelves lining every nook and cranny. A huge collection of books, video games, and toys filled the shelves. The bunk beds were covered with stuffed animals, and the ceiling was painted with glow-in-the-dark stars.*

1 Change this dialogue into action (1 sentence):

"What are you doing here?"
"I was going to ask you the same thing."
"Want to go exploring together?"
"Great idea!"
"Okay. Let's head into that cave!"

_____

_____

2 Change this dialogue into a description (2–3 sentences):

"That dress is beautiful!"
"It looks like it belongs to a princess!"
"Or a movie star!"
"I love the lace, ruffles, and sequins."

_____

_____

Name _____ Date _____

Too Much Talk–3

✏️ **Writer's Tip:** Remember that stories with all talk (no action or description) are hard for the reader to follow. Instead, use a balance of dialogue, action, and description.

DIRECTIONS: Read the dialogue below. Then change it to action or description.

> EXAMPLE: *"Bye, Mom."*
> *"Where are you going?"*
> *"I'm going to the beach."*
> *"Okay. Have a nice time!"*

> REVISION: (dialogue changed to action)
> *Mom and I said good-bye, and I left for the beach.*

1 Change this dialogue into action (1 sentence):

> **"There's Tim."**
> **"Hey, Tim. How's it going?"**
> **"Great."**
> **"Haven't seen you in a long time."**

_____

_____

_____

2 Change this dialogue into a description (2–3 sentences):

> **"This beach is nice!"**
> **"I love the sand dunes."**
> **"The water looks so blue."**
> **"Look at all the shells."**

_____

_____

_____

Name_____ Date _____

All Thought, No Action-1

 **Writer's Tip:** Authors can improve their writing by including the main character's thoughts and feelings. If the entire story takes place in the main character's head, however, the reader never gets to experience the setting or action. Be sure to include a balance of action, description, dialogue, thoughts, and feelings.

DIRECTIONS: Read the passage below, which consists of the main character's thoughts. Revise it by converting the thoughts into action and description.

EXAMPLE: *Hmmm . . . I think I'll go for a hike in the woods. Okay, I've got my gear. What a nice day it is out here. I'm almost there. Wow, these woods are beautiful. It's great to be out in nature like this.*

REVISION: *It was a great day for a hike in the woods. I put on my hiking boots and collected my gear. In minutes, I was wandering through the woods. The trees towered above me, and I listened to the chirping of birds and the rustling of the underbrush. I took a deep breath and smiled. It was great to be out in nature.*

Now it's your turn. How can you convert this passage into action and description?

I think it's a perfect day to head to the beach. I'd better bring my chair, bucket, and shovel. Oops, I almost forgot my sunscreen! Oh, I was right—it's beautiful here at the beach. I think I'll look for shells. There's a nice one!

_____

_____

_____

_____

_____

_____

Name _____ Date _____

All Thought, No Action–2

Writer's Tip: Authors can improve their writing by including the main character's thoughts and feelings. If the entire story takes place in the main character's head, however, the reader never gets to experience the setting or action. Be sure to include a balance of action, description, dialogue, thoughts, and feelings.

DIRECTIONS: Read the passage below, which consists of the main character's thoughts. Revise it by converting the thoughts into action and description.

EXAMPLE: *I hope we win the game. Oh no! That was a curve ball. That's one strike. Maybe this time I'll get a hit. Yikes! This pitcher is unbelievable. Two strikes. This is it, my last chance. Yes! I got a hit!*

REVISION: *I stood gripping the bat in my sweaty palms. The pitcher stepped back and hurled the ball at me. I took a deep breath and, at the last minute, the ball swerved to the right. "Strike!" yelled the umpire. I shook my head in disbelief and prepared for the next pitch. Woosh! The ball zoomed past me in a blur. "Strike two!" yelled the ump. This was it. The pitcher flung the ball over the plate, and I swung full force. I heard the crack of the bat connecting with the ball, and I watched the ball sail out of the park!*

Now it's your turn. How can you convert this passage into action and description?

I better get ready for this race. Okay, I'm at the starting line. Here we go! Uh-oh! I tripped. That slowed me down. Yes! I'm catching up! I can't believe it—I'm passing everyone. I'm getting really tired, but I have only a few steps to go. Here comes the finish line. I can't believe I won the race!

_____

_____

_____

_____

Getting Started

The ending of a story is crucial—it makes the final impression on the reader. The ending should sum up the events of the story or at least the changes brought about by the events. The ending needs to show the reader how the main character has grown or changed as a result of the experiences in the story.

Students are often uncertain about how to wrap up a story with style. They typically fall into a number of patterns and end their stories with:

So I went home and went to bed.
So that is the end of my story.
I woke up and realized it was all a dream.
Or simply an abrupt *THE END*

To help students avoid these pitfalls, show them a number of alternatives authors use to create effective endings. Some of the elements of a successful story ending are:

⚙ A memory of the main event

⚙ A decision resulting from the main event

⚙ An action that reflects an important decision

⚙ A feeling about what took place

⚙ A hope or wish

Generally, authors combine at least one or two of these elements in their endings. Read your students an effective ending of a story or book, such as E. B. White's classic, *Charlotte's Web.* Then analyze it and look for the use of the above techniques.

The activities in this section provide opportunities for students to revise story endings. Help students by generating questions, such as:

⚙ What would the main character remember most about the main event of this story? (a memory)

⚙ What decision might the main character make based on the story events? (a decision)

⚙ What might the reader do as a result of an important decision? (an action)

⚙ How would the main character feel about what took place? (a feeling)

⚙ What might the main character hope or wish for as a result of what took place? (a wish)

To start, model one of the activity sheets for the entire class and then allow students to proceed independently with other activity sheets.

Name_____ Date_____

End With Style-1

Writer's Tip: Writers use the ending of a story to show how the main character has grown or changed in some way as a result of his or her experiences. To do this, writers use a combination of techniques that include describing the main character's memories, decisions, actions, feelings, hopes, or wishes as a result of the events in the story.

DIRECTIONS: Underline the main character's memories in black, decisions in green, feelings in blue, and wishes or hopes in red.

As I looked up at the mountain, I knew that I would never forget my climbing adventure. It was hard to believe that only hours ago I was standing on the top, feeling exhilarated. My heart had been pounding loudly in my chest as I reached the peak, and I was filled with pride at my accomplishment. I knew at that moment that all of the months of training and preparation were well worth it. With one last look at the top, I picked up my gear and started home, hoping that I would have the opportunity to make it to the top once again. I decided that I would tackle an even higher mountain next time.

What do you suppose the story was about?

_____

_____

_____

_____

_____

Name _____   Date _____

End With Style-2

Writer's Tip: Writers use the ending of a story to show how the main character has grown or changed in some way as a result of his or her experiences. To do this, writers use a combination of techniques that include describing the main character's memories, decisions, actions, feelings, hopes, or wishes as a result of the events in the story.

DIRECTIONS: Underline the main character's memories in black, decisions in green, feelings in blue, and wishes or hopes in red.

The day we brought Buster home from the animal shelter was one of the happiest experiences I can remember. As he curled up on my lap on the car ride home, I decided that I had made a new best friend. That night, as Buster sniffed around the house and made himself at home, we all felt overjoyed to have a new member of the family. I can't imagine now what life would be like without him. I feel so lucky to have Buster, and I hope that a dog will always be a part of my life.

What do you suppose this story was about?

_____

_____

_____

_____

_____

Name _____   Date _____

Start an Ending

Writer's Tip: Writers use the ending of a story to show how the main character has grown or changed in some way as a result of his or her experiences. To do this, writers use a combination of techniques that include describing the main character's memories, decisions, actions, feelings, hopes, or wishes as a result of the events in the story.

DIRECTIONS: Write one sentence for each of these four types of endings (memory, feeling, hope or wish, and decision). Your sentence can be part of the ending of any story you wish. An example is provided for each type.

Memory
EXAMPLE: **I'll never forget the time I explored the old cave.**

_____

_____

Feeling
EXAMPLE: **I can still feel the chill tingling down my spine when I remember getting lost in the cave.**

_____

_____

Hope or Wish
EXAMPLE: **I hope that the next time I am out exploring, I don't find myself in a cave!**

_____

_____

Decision
EXAMPLE: **From that day on, I decided I would never go exploring alone.**

_____

_____

Super Story-Writing Strategies & Activities Scholastic Professional Books

Name _____ Date _____

Take Your Pick–1

Writer's Tip: Writers use the ending of a story to show how the main character has grown or changed in some way as a result of his or her experiences. To do this, writers use a combination of techniques that include describing the main character's memories, decisions, actions, feelings, hopes, or wishes as a result of the events in the story.

DIRECTIONS: Revise the story ending below. Use a combination of two or three techniques listed above to create a successful story ending.

EXAMPLE: *So that is my story about how I got away from the pirate.*

REVISION: *When I close my eyes, I can still see the sneering face of the pirate. I felt so relieved when I was finally able to free myself from his evil hold. I knew from that day on, I would never take my boat out to that part of the lagoon again.*

After my haunted house adventure, I went home and went to bed.

REVISION: _____

_____

_____

_____

_____

_____

_____

_____

Name_____ Date_____

Take Your Pick—2

Writer's Tip: Writers use the ending of a story to show how the main character has grown or changed in some way as a result of his or her experiences. To do this, writers use a combination of techniques that include describing the main character's memories, decisions, actions, feelings, hopes, or wishes as a result of the events in the story.

DIRECTIONS: Revise the story ending below. Use a combination of two or three techniques listed above to create a successful story ending.

EXAMPLE: *So that was the end of my big skiing adventure.*

REVISION: *I'll always remember my wild run down Devil's Peak. I can still feel the wind whipping across my face as I raced down the mountain at breakneck speeds. As I curl up by the fire, I hope that tonight's storm will bring plenty of snow for tomorrow's run.*

So that is the end of my story about getting caught in a thunderstorm.

REVISION:_____

_____

_____

_____

_____

_____

_____

Getting Started

After students have practiced the strategies in this book, they can use what they have learned to analyze and revise writing. To have them practice story analysis and revision, provide each student with a copy of the sample story on page 62 and a copy of the "Analyze This Story!" reproducible on page 63. Read the story aloud together, and then have students work through the questions on the reproducible. When they are finished, discuss the weaknesses in the story and brainstorm suggestions for revision. Here is a sample critique of the story, with suggestions for revision:

◎ The beginning of the story is dull and predictable.
(Instead, try action, exclamation or dialogue, thoughts or questions, or sounds.)

◎ The author uses a "grocery list" to describe the forest setting.
(Instead, separate each detail into its own sentence and use good sentence variety.)

◎ The author uses a "broken record" to describe the wizard.
(Instead, use different sentence subjects and active verbs to create sentence variety.)

◎ The main event (flying home) is summarized rather than fully described.
(Instead, break out each section of the summary by asking what the main character saw, heard, felt, exclaimed, thought, or wondered.)

◎ There is "wiretap" writing (too much talk) in the dialogue between the wizard and main character.
(Instead, use a better balance of dialogue, action, and description.)

◎ The ending is abrupt and unsatisfying.
(Instead, include the main character's memories, decisions, actions, feelings, hopes, and wishes as a result of the events in the story.)

Next, divide the class into groups of three or four students. Ask each group to revise one weak area of the draft. Be sure to assign a different section to each group so that each weakness will be revised. Circulate around the room and remind groups about the techniques they can use to revise their sections. (A sample revision is provided for reference at the end of this section, on page 64.)

Finally, substitute the revisions for each weak section. Compare the "before" and "after" versions. This activity provides students with a powerful picture of how revision can drastically improve a piece of writing.

Name _____ Date _____

The Wizard in the Cave

(Sample Story)

This is my story about the night I went exploring in the woods and met a wizard.

Carrying my flashlight, I set off into the deep, dark woods. The forest was creepy, mysterious, spooky, and full of tall trees. I tiptoed along, shivers running up and down my spine. I was determined to find the cave that I'd seen on the old map Grandpa had given me.

Suddenly, the ground seemed to slant down to the right. I pushed the bushes aside and discovered a small, overgrown trail. "This is it!" I whispered. "The trail leading to the cave!"

I walked cautiously down the trail as I peered into the darkness. Then I saw it—the mouth of the cave! Strange, I thought, there seemed to be a light flickering inside. I ducked down and crawled into the cave. My heart began pounding as I looked around. To my amazement, I was standing in some kind of chamber! And off to one side was a wizard!

The wizard had a long white beard. He had a blue cape and a purple robe. He had a tall pointy hat covered in sparkling stars. He had a wand in one hand and a crystal ball in the other.

"Who are you?" I asked.

"Willard the Wizard. What are you doing in my cave?"

"Exploring. Can I look around?"

"Yes. Would you like to learn some magic?"

"Cool! Can you teach me how to fly?"

"Yes."

"Great. Thanks!"

He handed me his wand, and I waved it around. I flew out of the cave and through the forest. In a blink of an eye, I found myself back in my bed, dizzy and confused. I wondered if the whole thing had been a dream. But no—there was my flashlight in my hand, and in the corner of my room stood the magic wand glowing in the dark. So I went to sleep.

THE END

Name _____ Date _____

Analyze This Story!

 *Writer's Tip:* Authors always read over what they've written with a critical eye, looking for ways to improve their writing. Then they go back and revise, often several times.

DIRECTIONS: Read "The Wizard in the Cave." The author has some great ideas, and with some revision this draft could become a very entertaining story. Help the author by analyzing this draft.

1 Circle the opening sentence in orange. Does it capture your attention and make you want to keep reading?

_____

2 Underline the description of the setting in red. What do we call this kind of description?

_____

3 Underline the description of the wizard in blue. What do we call this kind of description?

_____

4 Underline the dialogue between the wizard and the main character in black. Is this dialogue effective? _____ Why or why not?

_____

5 Draw a box around the main event. Is it fully elaborated or is it a summary?

_____

6 Circle the ending in green. Is this ending effective? _____ Why or why not?

_____

Name _____   Date _____

The Wizard in the Cave

(Sample Revision)

Hoot! Hoot! The sound of an owl cut through the deep, dark forest. I was out for an evening hike, using my flashlight to guide me on my way. Tall trees towered over me like giants. The thick underbrush loomed around me on all sides, casting spooky shadows across my path. In the distance, I heard the long, lonely howl of a coyote or perhaps a wolf. I tiptoed along, shivers running up and down my spine. I was determined to find the cave that I'd seen on the old map Grandpa had given me. I aimed my flashlight at the map and then looked around. Off to the right, the ground seemed to slant downward. I pushed the bushes aside and discovered a small, overgrown trail. "This is it!" I whispered. "The trail leading to the cave!"

Peering into the darkness, I walked cautiously down the trail. Then I saw it—the mouth of the cave! Strange, I thought, there seemed to be a light flickering inside. I ducked down and crawled into the cave. My heart began to pound as I looked around. To my amazement, I was standing in some kind of chamber. And off to one side stood a Wizard! His long white beard fell well below his waist. His tall, thick frame was draped in a bright blue satin cape. A velvety purple robe peeked out from beneath the cape and matched his tall pointed hat. The hat sparkled in the candlelight, and glitter seemed to float from the wand he held.

We greeted each other, and he kindly invited me to look around. When he asked me if I wanted to learn some magic, I jumped at the chance. I told him it had always been my dream to learn how to fly. He handed me his wand, and I waved it around. Suddenly, I was surrounded in a cloud of sparkles and felt my feet rise from the floor of the cave. I realized that I had sprouted two fluffy white wings that flapped gently behind me. The cave vanished in a blur as my wings carried me back outside. I got a bird's-eye view of the forest as I soared through the night sky. "Wheeee!" I yelled, frightening a whole treeful of roosting bats. In the blink of an eye, I found myself back home in bed, dizzy and confused. I wondered if I had dreamt the whole thing. But no—I was still clutching my flashlight, and in the corner of my room stood the magic wand glowing in the dark.

It is hard to believe what happened to me that night in the forest—it is something that I will never forget as long as I live. I feel so grateful to my Grandpa for giving me that map. He must have known it held a very special gift for me. I hope to meet the Wizard again someday so that I can thank him for my magical evening. In the meantime, I'll be practicing using my magic wand and planning my next hike to the secret cave deep in the woods.

THE END